Lighthouse
Psalms

Presented to:

_____

Presented by:

_____

Date:

_____

Lighthouse Psalms

*God's Gift
of Hope
and Direction*

Honor Books
Tulsa, Oklahoma

Lighthouse Psalms
ISBN 1-56292-805-8

Copyright 1999 by GRQ Ink, Inc.
381 Riverside Drive, Suite #250
Franklin, TN 37064

Published by Honor Books
P.O. Box 55388
Tulsa, OK 74155

Developed by GRQ Ink, Inc.
Manuscript written by W. Terry Whalin.
Cover and text design by Richmond & Williams
Composition by John Reinhardt Book Design

O LORD, you light my lamp.

My God turns my darkness into light

PSALM 18:28 GOD'S WORD

LIGHT SHINES ON THOSE WHO DO RIGHT

*Light is sown for the righteous,
and gladness for the upright in heart.*

PSALM 97:11 KJV

A s the sun dips behind the horizon, the old lighthouse begins to shine. The light sweeps across the sea and pierces through the darkness like a knife. The ship's crew sees the light in the early evening, then they notice it again in the middle of the night. Finally, in the early morning hours right before the dawn, they are once again reassured by its comforting light.

Do you ever feel alone on the sea of life? The light of God's love is constantly reaching out to you, just as the beam from the lighthouse reaches out to the ship at sea.

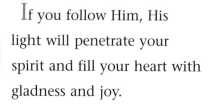

If you follow Him, His light will penetrate your spirit and fill your heart with gladness and joy.

I will be glad and rejoice in you;
I will sing praise to your name,
O Most High.

PSALM 9:2 NIV

But let the godly rejoice.
Let them be glad in God's presence.
Let them be filled with joy.

PSALM 68:3 NLT

You bestow on him blessings forever;
you make him glad with the joy of your presence.

PSALM 21:6 NRSV

GOD'S LIGHT LEADS US TO SAFETY

Oh, send out Your light and Your truth!
Let them lead me;
Let them bring me to Your holy hill
And to Your tabernacle.

PSALM 43:3 NKJV

The captain stands at the helm of his ship and points the bow toward the shore—at least he thinks it is the shore. A sudden storm is tossing the ship around in the dark, churning waters. It takes all the captain's strength to hold the wheel steady. *Where is the light?* he wonders as his eyes search for the horizon. Finally, hours later, the exhausted captain spots the beam from the lighthouse reaching out to him through the darkness. He breathes a sigh of relief because he knows that the light will guide him safely into the harbor.

When life's storms plunge you into darkness, you need the light of God's presence. It will guide you safely home.

Indeed, you are my rock and my fortress.
For the sake of your name, lead me and guide me.
Psalm 31:3 God's Word

The Lord is your protection;
you have made God Most High your place of safety.
Psalm 91:9 NCV

He will abide before God forever;
Appoint lovingkindness and truth, that they
may preserve him.
Psalm 61:7 NAS

For in the day of trouble
he will keep me safe in his dwelling;
he will hide me in the shelter of his tabernacle
and set me high upon a rock.
Psalm 27:5 NIV

A Burst of Light

When darkness overtakes him,
light will come bursting in.
He is kind and merciful.

PSALM 112:4 TLB

In the midst of the darkness and rough seas, the captain of a ship struggles to find his way without hitting the rocks that

hide right below the surface of the water. Then, the light from the lighthouse bursts from behind a jutting cliff and dissolves the darkness with a strong beam of light. The waters are transformed. They no longer hold the threat of disaster. The captain of the vessel smiles and brings his ship safely into the harbor.

The light of God's love can transform your dark and stormy waters. It can guide you away from the unseen rocks that can shipwreck your life.

God is kind and merciful. Follow His light and He will bring you safely through.

Hear my cry for mercy as I call to you for help,
as I lift up my hands toward your Most Holy Place.

PSALM 28:2 NIV

The LORD is just in all his ways,
and kind in all his doings.

PSALM 145:17 NRSV

Surely goodness and mercy shall follow me
all the days of my life: and I will dwell in
the house of the LORD for ever.

PSALM 23:6 KJV

LORD, remember me when you are
kind to your people;
help me when you save them.

PSALM 106:4 NCV

FOLLOW THE BEST PATH

The LORD says, "I will make you wise
and show you where to go.
I will guide you and watch over you."

PSALM 32:8 NCV

ᐧᐧᐧ

The shimmering light from the lighthouse beams across the ocean and reveals the rocks and sandbars. Without the beam, the shoreline would soon be littered with the bones of many ships. Every ship's captain knows that he must depend on the light from the lighthouse to bring his vessel safely into the harbor. He cannot hope to find the best path to safety without the light to guide him.

You may be searching for the right path for your life—the best path safely around the rocks and sandbars that will not leave your life in shipwreck.

God has promised to pour out His light on your life and show you the way. All you have to do is ask.

And I shall live before the Lord forever.
Oh, send your lovingkindness and truth
to guard and watch over me.

PSALM 61:7 TLB

The LORD keeps watch over you as you come and go,
both now and forever.

PSALM 121:8 NLT

Teach us to number each of our days
so that we may grow in wisdom.

PSALM 90:12 GOD'S WORD

SEARCH FOR GOD

Seek the LORD and his strength;
seek his presence continually.

PSALM 105:4 NRSV

Darkness is nothing more than the absence of light. When the light comes, it fills the darkness and illuminates our way. As the captain of a ship nears the vicinity of the lighthouse, he grows stronger and more confident. He knows that very soon the light from the lighthouse will fill the darkness before him and guide him to safety. He knows that the light will be there. He can depend on it.

Are you having trouble finding your way in the darkness? Walk toward the light of God's Word and presence. He may not choose to answer every question, but He will fill the darkness in your life with light so that you can walk confidently and without fear.

He promises that He will always be there. You can depend on it.

Show me your unfailing love
in wonderful ways.
You save with your strength
those who seek refuge
from their enemies.
PSALM 17:7 NLT

I will love You, O LORD, my strength.
The LORD is my rock and my
fortress and my deliverer;
My God, my strength, in whom I will trust;
My shield and the horn of my
salvation, my stronghold.
PSALM 18:1–2 NKJV

Constant Watch Care

I lay down and slept.
I woke up in safety,
for the LORD was watching over me.

PSALM 3:5 NLT

❧

The captain stands on the deck of his ship and looks out across the harbor. Everything is in order. A few hours earlier, his crew had anchored the ship, securing it for the night. As the gentle ocean breeze moves his hair, the captain studies the lighthouse in the distance. Now in the darkness, its beam of light sweeps back and forth across the ocean. As the captain heads below deck for the night, he knows that he will rest securely. The light from the lighthouse will stand watch as he sleeps.

When the cares of life weigh heavily on you, give them to God. He will stand watch over you throughout the night. You can depend on the light of His constant love.

I said, "I am about to fall,"
but, LORD, your love kept me safe.
PSALM 94:18 NCV

Set a guard, O LORD, over my mouth;
Keep watch over the door of my lips.
PSALM 141:3 NAS

For a thousand years in thy sight
are but as yesterday when it is past,
and as a watch in the night.
PSALM 90:4 KJV

Hold me up, that I may be safe
and have regard for your
statutes continually.
PSALM 119:117 NRSV

RESTING SAFELY IN GOD'S LOVE

*O God my Strength! I will sing
your praises, for you are my
place of safety.*

PSALM 59:9 TLB

A shipmate has been at his post for hours. Because of sickness among the crew, he has been required to take an extra long session at the ship's helm. His watch has been uneventful, but now he must steer the ship safely into the harbor. His shipmates, sleeping below, are depending on him to bring them all safely home. Just as exhaustion threatens to overwhelm him, his eyes find what they have been searching for—the light from the lighthouse. Now he knows that they will all be home soon, resting in the safety of the harbor.

The circumstances of your life may be pushing you to the point of exhaustion. Depend on the light of God's unfailing love to strengthen and encourage you. It will bring you safely home.

I have become an example to many people,
but you are my strong refuge.

Psalm 71:7 God's Word

You have not handed me over to my enemies
but have set me in a safe place.

Psalm 31:8 ncv

Wait for the Lord;
Be strong, and let your heart take courage;
Yes, wait for the Lord.

Psalm 27:14 nas

LIGHT GUIDES US AWAY FROM DESTRUCTION

Make my steps secure through your promise,
and do not let any sin control me.

PSALM 119:133 GOD'S WORD

❧

The piercing beam from the lantern atop the lighthouse chases away the darkness covering the surface of the water. The captains of the ships in the area depend on the light to help them avoid the rocks and sandbars that could sink their ships. They know that following the light is the only way for them to guide their vessels safely into the harbor.

There are also many dangers and pitfalls in this life. There are many opportunities to dash your life against the

rocks. But God has promised the light of His presence for all those who seek it.

———◦◦◦———

Ask God to shine His light into your life and guide you safely into the harbor. You can depend on Him.

And those who repay evil for good,
They oppose me, because
I follow what is good.
PSALM 38:20 NAS

The steps of a good man are
ordered by the LORD: and he
delighteth in his way.
PSALM 37:23 KJV

Happy are those who are strong in
the Lord, who want above all else to
follow your steps.
PSALM 84:5 TLB

A Tower of Strength

I call to you from the ends of the earth
when I am afraid.
Carry me away to a high mountain.

PSALM 61:2 NCV

Like a tower of strength, the ever-present lighthouse beams a constant light to guide ships to safety. That light comforts the crew and calms all their fears. It gives them the assurance that they will be able to pass safely to their destinations.

Is fear swallowing up your peace of mind and robbing you of your confidence? Just like the lighthouse that stands resolutely on the shore, sending its light to the passing ships, God is a tower of strength.

Put your trust in Him. Look to Him for help as you pass through the troubled waters. Your fears will flee, and you will know the sweet assurance of His unfailing love guiding you to safety.

But when I am afraid,
I put my trust in you.
O God, I praise your word.
I trust in God, so why should I be afraid?
What can mere mortals do to me?

PSALM 56:3–4 NLT

You will not be afraid of
the terror by night, or of the arrow that flies by day.

PSALM 91:5 NAS

Yea, though I walk through the valley of the
shadow of death, I will fear no evil:
for thou art with me; thy rod and thy staff they comfort me.

PSALM 23:4 KJV

Safety in God Alone

*I will say of the Lord, "He is my
refuge and my fortress;
My God, in Him I will trust."*

PSALM 91:2 NKJV

❧

A sudden storm tosses a small ship to and fro in the darkness. The captain of the vessel keeps his hands firmly on the wheel. He must keep his concentration on finding the harbor and guiding the ship to safety. As the winds increase, the captain wonders, *Will I make it back to the harbor?* Then he moves past a point of land, and the lighthouse comes into view, its beam guiding him to safety.

———❧———

Do you feel tossed about by unexpected situations in your life? Have you wondered where to turn for help? Put your trust in God, and He will lead you to safety in the harbor. He will shine the light of His love into your life and lead you to a refuge from the storm.

Protect me, O God,
because I take refuge in you.
PSALM 16:1 GOD'S WORD

LORD my God,
I trust in you for protection.
Save me and rescue me
from those who are chasing me.
PSALM 7:1 NCV

For the wicked will be destroyed,
but those who trust in the LORD
will possess the land.
PSALM 37:9 NLT

O my strength,
I will sing praises to you,
for you, O God, are my fortress,
the God who shows me
steadfast love.
PSALM 59:17 NRSV

STRAIGHT TO SAFETY

He led them on a road that went straight to an inhabited city.

PSALM 107:7 GOD'S WORD

❦

It takes great skill to handle a ship on the open sea. There is no highway to follow. There are no rules of the road—and no landmarks to show the way. On the open sea, the landscape looks the same in every direction. That's why, when a ship leaves the open sea and enters territorial waters, the lighthouse is so important. It sits on a hill, pointing the way to the safety of the harbor. It points the way home.

———⊷⊶———

God's love can serve as a light to guide you into a safe harbor. It gives context to the confusing landscape of your life and shows you which way to go. Once you learn to trust it, you can sail straight to safety.

He led me to a place of safety;
he rescued me because he delights in me.
PSALM 18:19 NLT

For thou art my rock and my fortress;
therefore for thy name's sake lead me,
and guide me.
PSALM 31:3 KJV

Now teach me good judgment as well
as knowledge. For your laws are my guide.
PSALM 119:66 TLB

Lead me in your truth, and teach me,
for you are the God of my salvation;
for you I wait all day long.
PSALM 25:5 NRSV

PROTECTION FOR THOSE WHO LOVE GOD

But let all who take refuge in you rejoice;
let them sing joyful praises forever.
Protect them, so all who love your
name may be filled with joy.

PSALM 5:11 NLT

~

The Cape Cod Lighthouse has been a firm fixture in the Massachusetts community since it was erected in 1797. This strong tower was rebuilt in 1853, then four years later it had to be replaced when the land near it crumbled into the sea. This 1857 reconstruction still stands today as a beacon of strength. Throughout the years, it has guarded the treacherous shores and allowed many ships to pass safely through the dark waters.

———⸎———

Like the Cape Cod light, God desires to be the light in your life. Throughout the years, He has been waiting for you to ask Him to shine His light across your dark waters and let Him lead you to safety.

Protect my life, and rescue me!
Do not let me be put to shame.
I have taken refuge in you.

PSALM 25:20 GOD'S WORD

In God is my salvation and my glory;
The rock of my strength,
And my refuge, is in God.

PSALM 62:7 NKJV

The LORD will protect you from all evil;
He will keep your soul.

PSALM 121:7 NAS

Be glad in the LORD, and rejoice,
ye righteous: and shout for joy,
all ye that are upright in heart.

PSALM 32:11 KJV

LIGHT CHASES THE DARKNESS

O Lord, you light my lamp.
My God turns my darkness into light.

PSALM 18:28 GOD'S WORD

～

The keeper of the lighthouse constantly maintains the huge light beam. With his care and concern, the light continues to burn brightly each evening. Those who travel along the rocky shoreline depend on him to keep the light moving, sweeping away the darkness, exposing any danger, and showing the way.

God wants to light your way and chase away the darkness in your life. He waits patiently and faithfully, sending His light out across the dark waters. Follow the light, and you will experience His protection and never-failing care. He wants to show you the way through your troubled waters.

———

He wants to light your path and guide you safely on your way. Open your heart to receive His light.

Light shines on the godly,
and joy on those who do right.
PSALM 97:11 NLT

The unfolding of your words gives light;
it imparts understanding to the simple.
PSALM 119:130 NRSV

Your words are a flashlight to
light the path ahead of me,
and keep me from stumbling.
PSALM 119:105 TLB

Light arises in the darkness
for the upright; He is gracious and
compassionate and righteous.
PSALM 112:4 NAS

A Refuge in Distress

But I will sing of your might;
I will sing aloud of your
steadfast love in the morning.
For you have been a fortress for me
and a refuge in the day of my distress.

The lamp from the towering lighthouse chases away the darkness and floods the area with light. Though the lighthouse itself is firmly anchored in its place of prominence in the harbor, the beam is always in motion, illuminating the water as it passes from one side of the harbor to the other.

God is like the lighthouse on the hill, never changing, always there. But the light of His love is always moving, searching the waters, reaching out to those who are distressed and need to find refuge in the harbor.

In your day of distress, let the light of God's love illuminate your troubled waters and show you which way to go.

God is our refuge and strength,
an ever-present help in times of trouble.

PSALM 46:1 GOD'S WORD

In my distress, I said,
"God cannot see me!"
But you heard my prayer when I cried out to you for help.

PSALM 31:22 NCV

I called on the LORD in distress;
The LORD answered me and set me in a broad place.

PSALM 118:5 NKJV

Be thou to me a rock of
habitation, to which I may continually come;
Thou hast given commandment to save me,
For Thou art my rock and my fortress.

PSALM 71:3 NAS

God's Preservation

Thou, O Lord, wilt keep them;
Thou wilt preserve him
from this generation forever.

PSALM 12:7 NAS

A lighthouse is a tower of strength, sending out its beam of light throughout the dark and dangerous night. Ships depend on it to guide them safely through the dark waters and bring them safely into the harbor. They count on that constant, solitary beam to preserve them from harm.

As you look to God, the light of His presence will preserve your life and lead you safely to your destination. You will be safe as you journey through the uncertain waters of life.

Place your trust in God's constant love, and call on Him to guide you safely through. He is waiting, ready to help. He will not disappoint you.

Keep me as the apple of the eye,
hide me under the shadow of thy wings.
PSALM 17:8 KJV

I will keep on expecting you to help me.
I praise you more and more.
PSALM 71:14 TLB

Do not, O LORD, withhold your mercy from me;
let your steadfast love and your faithfulness
keep me safe forever.
PSALM 40:11 NRSV

Hear my voice in accordance with your love;
preserve my life, O LORD, according to your laws.
PSALM 119:149 NIV

O LORD, keep me alive for the sake of your name.
Because you are righteous, lead me out of trouble.
PSALM 143:11 GOD'S WORD

God's Protection Goes with You

He will put his angels in charge of you
to protect you in all your ways.

PSALM 91:11 GOD'S WORD

∽

The captain takes off his hat and smooths his graying hair as he stands on the bridge of his ship, guiding it toward the harbor in the early evening. A young mate standing with him spots the beam from a distant lighthouse. "Ever had any close calls, Captain?" the mate asks. "Many times," the captain responds. "I've always followed the light from the lighthouse, and it keeps me from running into any rocks or sandbars just below the surface of the water."

Just as the captain places his trust in the lighthouse, you can place your trust in God. Sure, there will be close calls, but as long as you trust in the light, He will protect and preserve your life.

You are my rock and my protection.
For the good of your name, lead me and guide me.
Set me free from the trap they set for me,
because you are my protection.
I give you my life.
Save me, LORD, God of truth.

PSALM 31:3–5 NCV

Rescue me from my enemies, O God.
Protect me from those who have come to destroy me.

PSALM 59:1 NLT

The LORD will protect you from all evil;
He will keep your soul.

PSALM 121:7 NAS

I have declared my ways,
and thou heardest me:
teach me thy statutes.

PSALM 119:26 NJV

PROTECTION FROM EVIL

Keep me as the apple of the eye,
hide me under the shadow of thy wings,
From the wicked that oppress me,
from my deadly enemies, who compass me about.

PSALM 17:8–9 KJV

The lighthouse stands on the hill overlooking the harbor in good weather and in bad. It keeps its vigil under sunny skies and through daunting storms. The ship's crew faces many uncertainties—crushing winds, strong tides, blinding rain. But no matter what the circumstances, the lighthouse stands its ground. Its strong beam is the one sure thing on which the ship's crew can depend.

God promises that the light of His presence will shine brightly in your life whether you are being tossed about in the angry waves or sailing smoothly along to your destination. His protection will keep you no matter what evil is pressing in on you.

When you place your trust in Him, He will keep you safe through the storm.

Assign me Godliness and Integrity as my
bodyguards, for I expect you to protect me.

PSALM 25:21 TLB

But let all who take refuge in you be glad;
let them ever sign for joy.
Spread your protection over them,
that those who love your name may rejoice in you.

PSALM 5:11 NIV

Rescue me from my enemies, O LORD.
I come to you for protection.
Teach me to do your will, because you are my God.
May your good Spirit lead me on level ground.

PSALM 143:9-10 GOD'S WORD

God stands beside you to protect you.
He will strike down many kings in the
day of his anger.

PSALM 110:5 TLB

GOD'S CERTAIN DELIVERANCE

Save me from them! Deliver my life
from their power! Oh, let it never be
said that I trusted you in vain!

PSALM 25:20 TLB

∽

The wind rushes across the bow of the ship. The turbulent waves rock it back and forth. The captain wrinkles his brow and stays the course. The ocean grows rough as the captain scans the horizon, searching for the lighthouse. He can sense the power of the wind as it tears at his hands, face, and clothing. As he grips the wheel, the darkness suddenly explodes with light. The danger is almost over. He can now steer his ship safely into

the harbor.

Have gale-force winds and turbulent waves come crashing into your life? Have you wondered if you will be able to weather the storm? Place your trust in God.

The light of His love can bring you safely through any storm.

Arise, O LORD; save me, O my God!
For Thou hast smitten all my enemies on the cheek;
Thou hast shattered the teeth of the wicked.
Salvation belongs to the LORD;
Thy blessing be upon
Thy people!
PSALM 3:7–8 NAS

Save thy people, and bless thine inheritance:
feed them also, and lift them up for ever.
PSALM 28:9 KJV

Turn, O LORD, and deliver me;
save me because of your unfailing love.
PSALM 6:4 NIV

Reach down from heaven and rescue me;
deliver me from deep waters,
from the power of my enemies.
PSALM 144:7 NLT

A Firm Foundation

Be my place of safety where I can always come.
Give the command to save me,
because you are my rock and my
strong, walled city.

Psalm 71:3 NCV

⸎

The waves beat constantly against the rocks along the shore, pounding, sliding, and then falling back into the sea. Above the rocks, the lighthouse stands at the point, and

throughout the night its beam never wavers. Lighthouses are built to weather centuries of pounding and remain firmly anchored to their rock foundations.

When the waves come crashing down on your life, turn to God. He is your firm foundation—your rock-hard refuge. He will not be moved by the crashing waves. He will stand strong against any storm.

He will provide safety and protection for you as you place your trust in Him. He will be your firm foundation.

From the ends of the earth,
I will cry to you for help,
for my heart is overwhelmed.
Lead me to the towering rock of safety.

PSALM 61:2 NLT

Save me, O God, by Your name,
And vindicate me by Your strength.

PSALM 54:1 NKJV

Yes, you are my Rock
and my fortress;
honor your name
by leading me out of this peril.

PSALM 31:3 TLB

PROTECTION AT DAYBREAK

God is in that city, and so it will not be shaken.
God will help her at dawn.

PSALM 46:5 NCV

❧

The fisherman wipes his hand across his brow. Throughout the night, he and his crew have worked the waters, casting their nets and pulling in fish. The fisherman is thankful for a good catch and a good night's work. Now as the dawn breaks over the horizon, he heads toward home. As the boat rounds the point, the fisherman looks with respect at the ancient lighthouse. Its beam of light sweeps through the darkness, guiding his weary body home.

Are you weary like the fisherman? Have you been working hard throughout the night? Place your trust in God. The light of His presence will lead you to a place where your heart and mind can find rest.

You heard their cries for help and saved them.
They put their trust in you and were
never disappointed.

PSALM 22:5 NLT

I have set the LORD continually before me;
Because He is at my right hand,
I will not be shaken.

PSALM 16:8 NAS

In the farthest corners of the earth
the glorious acts of god shall startle
everyone. The dawn and sunset shout for joy!

PSALM 65:8 TLB

PROTECTION FROM EVIL PLANS

Hide me from those who plan wicked things,
from that gang who does evil.

PSALM 64:2 NCV

A lighthouse is an unusual structure in many ways. For one thing, it has only one door that serves both as entrance and as exit. The light atop the lighthouse can be reached only by entering a single door and climbing a circular staircase. The single doorway is actually intended to make the lighthouse more defensible. It is easy for the keeper of the lighthouse to defend the single entrance against intruders who would want to destroy its light to advance their own purposes.

When you place your trust in God, He will defend you from the evil plans of those who would try to destroy your life. He will hide you safely inside a strong tower with a single entrance, and His mighty hand of protection will be ever guarding the door.

For he will hide me in his shelter
in the day of trouble;
he will conceal me under the cover of his tent;
he will set me high on a rock.

PSALM 27:5 NRSV

My enemies spy on me.
Pay them back with evil.
Destroy them with your truth!

PSALM 54:5 GOD'S WORD

The LORD is known by his justice;
the wicked are ensnared by the
work of their hands.

PSALM 9:16 NIV

Save me from my enemies, LORD;
I run to you to hide me.

PSALM 143:9 NLT

Rescued from Every Trap

Surely He shall deliver you from
the snare of the fowler
And from the perilous pestilence.

PSALM 91:3 NKJV

The icy ocean water pounds the shore. The wind and rain are fierce, but several ships continue with caution through the night. The captains and their mates keep watch because along these treacherous shores danger lurks just below the surface of the water. One wrong move and their vessels could be destroyed. They watch for the beam from the faithful lighthouse, knowing that once they come within its reach, the traps and snares will be revealed and they will be able to pass safely to their destinations.

Are you concerned about the dangers hidden along your path? Place your trust in God, and the light of His presence will bring you safely to your destination by helping you steer away from the rocks that threaten to destroy your life.

Reach down from heaven and rescue me;
deliver me from deep waters, from the
power of my enemies.
Psalm 144:7 TLB

Turn, O Lord, save my life;
deliver me for the sake of your steadfast love.
Psalm 6:4 NRSV

O keep my soul, and deliever me:
let me not be ashamed;
for I put my trust in thee.
Psalm 25:20 KJV

Set me free from the trap
they set for me,
because you are
my protection.
Psalm 31:4 NCV

HOPE AND PROTECTION RESTORED

*May integrity and uprightness
preserve me,
for I wait for you.*

PSALM 25:21 NRSV

The lighthouse towers above the water. From a distance, it seems to those who pass by to be pointing toward the sky. It was built to withstand strong winds and crashing waves. The crews on the passing ships have learned to trust in the integrity of the lighthouse, to depend on its faithful beam as it passes across the surface of the water again and again.

God's integrity is certain. It never fails. You can depend on it as you pass through the troubled waters of life. He will give you hope and protection when you place your trust in Him.

His Word promises that you will never be disappointed.

You defend my integrity,
and you set me in your presence forever.
PSALM 41:12 GOD'S WORD

May integrity and uprightness protect me,
because my hope is in you.
PSALM 25:21 NIV

My shield is with God,
Who saves the upright in heart.
PSALM 7:10 NAS

Wait on the LORD;
Be of good courage,
And He shall strengthen your heart;
Wait, I say, on the LORD!
PSALM 27:14 NKJV

Assign me Godliness
and Integrity as my bodyguards,
for I expect you to protect me.
PSALM 25:21 TLB

Promised Protection

Argue my case; take my side!
Protect my life as you promised.

Psalm 119:154 NLT

∽

Night after night, the light from the lighthouse sweeps across the surface of the water and guides the ships to safety in the harbor. Fishermen depend on its beam to illuminate the waters and lead them home. Even in the daylight, a lighthouse serves as a landmark for those passing by.

God is more reliable than the most dependable lighthouse.

He has promised to protect those who place their trust in Him. He has promised to lead and guide those who look to Him for safe passage through the waters of life.

⸺

For those who trust in Him, God is there, quietly pointing the way even in the daylight. You can depend on Him to show you the way.

Just as the mountains surround and protect
Jerusalem, so the Lord surrounds and protects his people.
PSALM 125:2 TLB

This God—his way is perfect;
the promise of the LORD proves true;
he is a shield for all who take refuge in him.
PSALM 18:30 NRSV

The LORD is on my side; I will
not fear: what can man do unto me?
PSALM 118:6 KJV

He always remembers his promise,
the word that he commanded for a thousand generations,
the promise that he made to Abraham,
and his sworn oath to Isaac.
PSALM 105:8–9 GOD'S WORD

Protect me, God,
because I trust in you.
PSALM 16:1 NCV

"Because he loves me," says the LORD, "I will rescue him;
I will protect him, for he acknowledges my name."
PSALM 91:14 NIV

LIGHT REVEALS TRUTH

Send me your light and truth to guide me.
Let them lead me to your holy mountain,
to where you live.

PSALM 43:3 NCV

A s a fisherman cast his nets in the deep waters, the wind suddenly shifted and the boat began to rock to and fro. Knowing the dangerous nature of the waters from which he drew his

livelihood, the fisherman hauled up his anchor and pointed the bow of his ship toward land. As he gripped the wheel of the craft, his eyes scanned the horizon. *Where is that light?* he muttered to himself. This fisherman had learned to trust the light to guide him home. Soon he saw the familiar landmark and guided his vessel safely back to shore.

When you feel the winds shifting in your life and find yourself being tossed about by the waves, look to God. He will lead you safely to the shore.

For this is God,
Our God forever and ever;
He will be our guide
Even to death.

PSALM 48:14 NKJV

The Lord's promise is sure. He speaks
no careless word; all he says is purest
truth, like silver seven times refined.

PSALM 12:6 TLB

From the end of the earth I call to you,
when my heart is faint.
Lead me to the rock that is higher than I.

PSALM 61:2 NRSV

I will instruct thee and teach thee
in the way which thou shalt go:
I will guide thee with mine eye.

PSALM 32:8 KJV

Showing the Way

O Lord, lead me in Thy
righteousness because of my foes;
Make Thy way straight before me.

Psalm 5:8 nas

The water shimmers in the afternoon sun as a ship glides through the smooth ocean. The captain of the vessel stands on the bridge reveling in the smell of the salt air and the gentle breeze. *It is perfect weather for moving along the coast and heading into the harbor,* he tells himself. As the vessel rounds the point, the captain sees a firm fixture on the point—the lighthouse. Day or night, the captain knows the lighthouse is always there to see him safely to his destination.

Whether you face smooth sailing or rough seas, God is always there looking after you, ready to show you the way to your next destination. Day or night, He is always there to bring you safely home.

He led them on a straight road
to a city where they could live.
Let them give thanks to the LORD for his love
and for the miracles he does for people.

PSALM 107:7–8 NCV

Teach me how to live, O LORD.
Lead me along the path of honesty,
for my enemies are waiting for me to fall.

PSALM 27:11 NLT

From the end of the earth I will cry to You,
When my heart is overwhelmed;
Lead me to the rock that is higher than I.

PSALM 61:2 NKJV

Lighting the Path

Lead me in thy truth, and teach me:
for thou art the God of my salvation;
on thee do I wait all the day.

PSALM 25:5 KJV

∽

The channel around the lighthouse is filled with danger. Huge rocks rise up from the ocean floor and lurk beneath the surface. The captain watches vigilantly as he steers the ship through the treacherous waters. As night falls, he can no longer count on the sun's light to help him see the dangers ahead. Now he must depend on the beam from the lighthouse, which stands on a point overlooking the shoreline. Its dependable light cuts through the darkness and illuminates the water in the ship's path.

————

When the truth becomes difficult to see in this uncertain world, turn to God. The light of His love will shine on the path before you and allow you to see the dangers in your path.

Lead me in the path of your commandments,
for I delight in it.

PSALM 119:35 NRSV

My honor and salvation come from God.
He is my mighty rock and my protection.

PSALM 62:7 NCV

You guide me with your counsel,
and afterward you will take me into glory.

PSALM 73:24 NIV

A TOWERING ROCK OF SAFETY

From the end of the earth I call to you,
when my heart is faint.
Lead me to the rock that is higher than I.

PSALM 61:2 NRSV

❧

As the sun dips below the horizon, the keeper of the lighthouse climbs the spiral staircase to the top. He turns on the light, and the beam begins to scour the surface of the water. Throughout the night the light circles, keeping its nightly vigil for the ships that pass by. The light of God's love is always there, making a way for you—when your heart is faint and your body is tired, in times of rejoicing and in times of deep sorrow.

———✺———

No matter what time of the night it is, God's love is there to see you safely through. Look for it. Depend on it. Let it give you safe passage through the dark night. It will not fail you.

Turn your ear toward me.
Rescue me quickly.
Be a rock of refuge for me,
a strong fortress to save me.

PSALM 31:2 GOD'S WORD

He is my rock and my salvation.
He is my defender;
I will not be defeated.

PSALM 62:2 NCV

Create in me a pure heart, O God,
and renew a steadfast spirit within me.

PSALM 51:10 NIV

The LORD lives, and blessed be my rock;
And exalted be the God of my salvation.

PSALM 18:46 NAS

Safety Permits Joy

Therefore my heart is glad,
and my glory rejoices;
My flesh also will dwell
securely.

PSALM 16:9 NAS

As the lamp on the top of the lighthouse begins its vigil, sweeping across the open sea, it brings a feeling of security and comfort to those passing by in ships. The ships in the area depend on the faithful work of the lighthouse. Without its ever-present beam, they would be able to travel only in the daytime or would have to risk the uncertainty of deeper water.

Without the light of God's presence, no one can feel safe passing through the treacherous waters of this life.

Put your faith in God and allow Him to light your way. You will be able to rest securely and your heart will rejoice as you experience the security of His constant vigil. He will see you safely to your destination.

For our heart shall rejoice in him,
because we have trusted in his holy name.
PSALM 33:21 KJV

I will be glad, yes, filled with joy
because of you. I will sing your praises,
O Lord God above all gods.
PSALM 9:2 TLB

The instructions of the LORD are correct.
They make the heart rejoice.
The command of the LORD is radiant.
It makes the eyes shine.
PSALM 19:8 GOD'S WORD

THE ROAD TO EVERLASTING LIFE

See if there is any bad thing in me.
Lead me on the road to everlasting life.

PSALM 139:24 NCV

In the darkness, the light from the lighthouse penetrates and moves across the surface of the water. As the light passes across the water, it reveals rocks or any potential danger that is lurking undetected in the water. The light guides all those who pass by to safety.

As you pass through the waters of life, allow the searchlight of God's truth to shine into your heart. It will reveal the dangers that can destroy your life. Along with God's light comes His everlasting peace. You will know how to correct your course. You will be able to see those obstacles that could keep you from happiness and fulfillment before they are able to bring you harm.

Teach me how to live, O LORD.
Lead me along the path of honesty,
for my enemies are waiting for me to fall.
PSALM 27:11 NLT

Thou wilt make known to me the path of life;
In Thy presence is fulness of joy;
In Thy right hand
there are pleasures forever.
PSALM 16:11 NAS

Lead me; teach me; for you are the
God who gives me salvation.
I have no hope except in you.
PSALM 25:5 TLB

FINDING FIRM FOOTING

Help me to do your will, for you
are my God. Lead me in good paths,
for your Spirit is good.

PSALM 143:10 TLB

∽

There are two pathways to the lighthouse, which sits on the point overlooking the harbor. The keeper of the lighthouse has kept one of the paths clean and clear throughout the years. He has even added stones to make it accessible in all types of weather. The second path winds through the rocks. Vines have grown up on the walkway and pose a danger to anyone who tries to climb the path to the peak. Each person must make his or her own choice.

―――⸻―――

You may be facing a difficult choice in your life. You may need God's help to choose the right path. Lay your choices at God's feet and ask Him to help you choose the path that will bring you safely to the top.

You make a wide path for me to walk on
so that my feet do not slip.
PSALM 18:36 GOD'S WORD

You have made known to me the path of life;
you will fill me with joy in your presence,
with eternal pleasures at your right hand.
PSALM 16:11 NIV

But giving thanks is a sacrifice that truly honors me.
If you keep to my path,
I will reveal to you the salvation of God.
PSALM 50:23 NLT

Lead me in the path of your commands,
because that makes me happy.
PSALM 119:35 NCV

FLORENCE

DIRECTING EVERY DETAIL

*The steps of a man are
established by the LORD;
And He delights in his way.*

PSALM 37:23 NAS

∽

The captain of a ship looks out across the water. He gains confidence as the light illuminates the path before him. He is grateful for the light and glad that it doesn't move about randomly but always in the same direction and in a timely rotation.

We all depend on the orderliness God has placed in His creation. It is good to know that the sun will come up in the morning at a precise and calculated time. Even if the clouds block its rays, we know that the sun is still there.

———

God has a plan for your life. A plan that you can count on, even when storm clouds drift through. Ask Him, and He will show you the way.

Righteousness will go before him,
and will make a path for his steps.
P SALM 85:13 NRSV

Teach me thy way, O L ORD,
and lead me in a plain path,
because of mine enemies.
P SALM 27:11 KJV

God arms me with strength
and makes my way perfect.
P SALM 18:32 G OD'S W ORD

A Sure and Certain Path

Make my steps secure through your promise,
and do not let any sin control me.

PSALM 119:133 GOD'S WORD

A group of fishermen are at work. Throughout the night, they throw their nets into the water and bring them back into the vessel. In the early morning hour just before the dawn, they empty their nets for the last time and head for home. Without the light that guides them safely through the dark waters, they would not be able to make a living as fishermen. Each trip might be their last.

The light of God's presence in your life can make it possible for you to do many things that you would not be able to do otherwise. It will lead you away from the pitfalls that can keep you from realizing God's perfect plan for your life and will make your steps secure.

He took me to a safe place.
Because he delights in me, he saved me.
PSALM 18:19 NCV

The children of your people
will live in security.
Their children's children
will thrive in your presence.
PSALM 102:28 NLT

The steps of a man are established by the LORD;
And He delights in his way.
PSALM 37:23 NAS

SEARCH FOR JOY AND GLADNESS

But may all who seek you
rejoice and be glad in you;
may those who love your salvation
say continually, "Great is
the LORD!"

PSALM 40:16 NRSV

The keeper of the lighthouse knows that he has a great responsibility. The very lives of those who pass through the rocky waters below are in his hands. Therefore, he spends the day diligently checking and rechecking for anything that could keep the light from burning brightly throughout the night. Everything seems to be in place, but he continues to search and finds a frayed wire that needs to be replaced. He replaces the wire and, as the sun begins to set, he rests confidently, knowing that the ships will pass safely for another night.

God knows all about you, and He is always at work urging you to search inside and repair anything that might keep His light from shining brightly on your path.

I will be glad and rejoice in thy mercy:
for thou hast considered my trouble;
thou hast known my soul in adversities.

PSALM 31:7 KJV

Let all who seek you rejoice and be glad because of you.
Let those who love your salvation continually say,
"God is great!"

PSALM 70:4 GOD'S WORD

I do not hide your righteousness in my heart;
I speak of your faithfulness and salvation.
I do not conceal your love and your truth from
the great assembly.

PSALM 40:10 NIV

Then I will rejoice in the LORD.
I will be glad because he rescues me.

PSALM 35:9 NLT

The humble have seen it
and are glad;
You who seek God,
let your heart revive.

PSALM 69:32 NAS

A Night Rescue

In my distress I called to the Lord;
I cried to my God for help.
From his temple he heard my voice;
my cry came before him, into his ears.

PSALM 18:6 NIV

A distress call goes out from a tiny vessel struggling to stay afloat in the stormy darkness. As the call is received, the keeper of the light-house searches the waters below from his high perch. Hour after hour, he faithfully scans the surface of the water for any sign of the tiny craft. Suddenly he sees it perched on the tip of a wave, and he rushes down the path to alert the rescuers on the shore. Soon the crew and their boat are safely on shore.

Do you feel like you are hopelessly lost in a storm? Call out to God. He will hear you and bring you safely through the troubled waters of your life. Put your trust in Him.

Search for the LORD and his strength.
Always seek his presence.
PSALM 105:4 GOD'S WORD

Be glad that you are his;
let those who seek the LORD
be happy.
PSALM 105:3 NCV

My soul will boast in the LORD;
let the afflicted hear and rejoice.
PSALM 34:2 NIV

You know what I long for, Lord;
you hear my every sigh.
PSALM 38:9 NLT

And I will walk at liberty,
For I seek Your precepts.
PSALM 119:45 NKJV

Search for Strength

Search for the LORD and for his strength,
and keep on searching.

PSALM 105:4 NLT

∽

Each night without fail, the faithful beam from the lighthouse searches the waters below. It stands as a guide for passing ships, a searchlight for ships in peril, and a warning of dangerous rocks and sandbars to vessels approaching the harbor. It is a tower of strength for those who depend upon its beam to light their way.

───

If you are searching for a tower of strength in your life—someone who will guide you safely through the troubled waters

of life, someone who will rescue you in your time of distress, someone who will warn you away from the obstacles that lay hidden in your path—open your heart to God. He will be there when you need Him most.

Now I know that the LORD
saves His anointed;
He will answer him from
His holy heaven,
With the saving strength of His right hand.
Some boast in chariots, and some in horses;
But we will boast in the name of the LORD, our God.

PSALM 20:6–7 NAS

The LORD is my light and my salvation;
Whom shall I fear?
The LORD is the strength of my life;
Of whom shall I be afraid?

PSALM 27:1 NKJV

O Lord, don't stay away. O God my Strength,
hurry to my aid. Rescue me from death;
spare my precious life from all these evil men.

PSALM 22:19–20 TLB

Summon your might, O God;
show your strength, O God, as
you have done for us before.

PSALM 68:28 NRSV

God Makes My Way Safe

God is my protection.
He makes my way free from fault.

PSALM 18:32 NCV

∽

The tower on the hillside near the ocean is always present. At the top of the tower, a light swings into action every evening. As it moves over the ocean surface, the light cuts through the darkness and provides the help that vessels need to navigate the water. The light reveals any potential dangers and gives those in the ships below a solid measure of comfort and protection.

———

God can bring comfort and protection to your life. He can guide you safely through any storm, and He will be your constant source of strength if you will only ask Him. Open your heart to His gentle care. He will not fail you.

But let all who take refuge
in you be glad;
let them ever sing for joy.
Spread your protection over them,
that those who love your name may rejoice in you.

PSALM 5:11 NIV

The LORD will protect you from all evil;
He will keep your soul.
The LORD will guard your going out
and your coming in from this time
forth and forever.

PSALM 121:7–8 NAS

You are their strength. What glory!
Our power is based on your favor!
Yes, our protection is from the Lord
himself and he, the Holy One of Israel,
has given us our king.

PSALM 89:17–18 TLB

TEST MY HEART

Search me, O God, and know my heart;
Try me, and know my anxieties.

PSALM 139:23 NKJV

෴

As the light from the lighthouse sweeps across the water, it has really just one solitary task—to dispel the darkness and reveal the hidden dangers in the murky waters below. The result is safety and protection for the ships that travel along the shoreline.

God's light can serve a similar function in your heart and life. When you open your heart to Him, the light of His love reveals dangers and obstacles that lay hidden below the surface.

Ask God to search your heart and help you see those things that could lead you to unwise choices and destructive behaviors. His light is always gentle and leads to safety and truth.

O Lord, you have examined my heart and
know everything about me. You know when
I sit or stand. When far away you know
my every thought.

PSALM 139:1–2 TLB

Prove me, O LORD, and try me;
test my heart and mind.
For your steadfast love
is before my eyes,
and I walk in faithfulness to you.

PSALM 26:2–3 NRSV

Search for the LORD and his strength.
Always seek his presence.

PSALM 105:4 GOD'S WORD

GOD IS ALWAYS THERE

Your faithfulness continues
through all generations;
You established the earth, and it endures.

PSALMS 119:90 NIV

❧

It is not yet noon, and the water sparkles as the sun beats down on it. A ship's captain guides his ship toward the shore. Today it is easy to see the obstacles in the ship's path. Nevertheless, he looks toward the tower in the distance and whispers a word of thanksgiving. Whether he needs the light or not, it is always present.

You may feel that your life is moving along just fine. But the day will come when you do need the light that beams down from the lighthouse. When you do, it will be there for you. God's love means that you will never have to cross the troubled waters of life alone in the darkness.

I cry out to God Most High,
to the God who does everything for me.
He sends help from heaven
and saves me.
He punishes those who chase me.
God sends me his love and truth.

PSALM 57:2-3 NCV

The righteous cry and the LORD hears,
And delivers them out of all their troubles.
The LORD is near to the brokenhearted,
And saves those who are crushed in spirit.

PSALM 34:17-18 NAS

THE LIGHT OF GOD'S WORDS

The unfolding of your words gives light;
it imparts understanding to the simple.

PSALM 119:130 NRSV

Water swirls and crashes against a rock formation along the shore. Nearby, the light from a lighthouse patrols the area, warning any passing ships of the potential dangers below. Without the light, the ships would not know to steer clear of the precarious formation.

When you read God's words, recorded in the Bible, they will bring His light to bear on your life by providing simple understanding and guidance. Don't let your life be shipwrecked by those things you cannot see. Let the light of God's words show you the way.

Receive God's wisdom and truth. It's the only way to keep your life off the rocks and sailing peacefully away from danger.

You made me and formed me with your hands.
Give me understanding so I can learn
your commands.

PSALM 119:73 NCV

For with you is the fountain of life;
in your light we see light.
Continue your love to those who know you,
your righteousness to the upright in heart.

PSALM 36:9–10 NIV

Blessed is the people that know the
joyful sound: they shall walk, O LORD,
in the light of thy countenance.

PSALM 89:15 KJV

Increased Power

He will take all power away from the wicked,
but the power of good people will grow.

Psalm 75:10 ncv

⁓

The powerful light from the lighthouse sweeps the water throughout the night. Without the beam, many ships would be crushed on the rocks below. The keeper of the lighthouse holds the lives of many in his hands. Along with that power, he also carries great responsibility. He must faithfully see that the light is always there when it is needed.

The affairs of this world are often in conflict with the ways of God. We all know that there are wicked people who hold great power over the lives of many.

Nevertheless, if you want God's power in your life—the power of His wisdom and truth—practice reaching out to others and helping them see the dangerous rocks that threaten their lives.

Say to God, "How awesome are your deeds!
So great is your powerthat your enemies cringe before you.
All the earth bows down to you;
they sing praise to you, they sing praise to your name."

PSALM 66:3–4 NIV

But I will sing of Your power;
Yes, I will sing aloud of Your mercy in the morning;
For You have been my defense
And refuge in the day of my trouble.

PSALM 59:16 NKJV

God's Favor

*Let your favor shine again upon your
servant; save me just because you are so kind!*

Everything is working well in
the lighthouse. The huge beam
is lighting a path for the ships,
and the keeper is curled up
with a good book. The winds
look calm, and the evening
promises to be uneventful. But
suddenly, the electricity in the
area goes down and the light vanishes. But only for a second. The keeper swings into action and
quickly moves a generator into place. He always has a backup
power source at hand. The passing ships are depending on him.

There are no power breakdowns with the light of God's
love. He has vast resources, and He uses them to make sure you
will never be without His light to guide you through the dark
waters of life.

For the LORD God is a sun and shield;
the LORD bestows favor and honor;
no good thing does he withhold
from those whose walk is blameless.

PSALM 84:11 NIV

They rejoice all day long in your wonderful reputation.
They exult in your righteousness.
You are their glorious strength.
Our power is based on your favor.

PSALM 89:16–17 NLT

Show Us Better Times

*Many people ask,
"Who will give us anything good?"
Lord, be kind to us.*

Psalm 4:6 ncv

The light from the lighthouse shines down on the water tonight as it does every night, keeping its constant vigil. Tonight the water is calm and a soft breeze is blowing. All is well. But without the light, it would be easy for those who are passing by to imagine a great many obstacles in the dark waters ahead.

Have you ever wondered if God really loves and cares for you? Do you worry about what disaster could be lurking in the waters ahead?

Let the light of God's love shine into your heart. Then you will be certain of His constant love and protection. His light will assure you that all is well.

Come, O Lord, and make me well.
In your kindness save me.
PSALM 6:4 TLB

The LORD is righteous in everything he does;
he is filled with kindness.
The LORD is close to all who call on him,
yes, to all who call on him sincerely.
PSALM 145:17–18 NLT

Good and upright is the LORD;
therefore he instructs sinners in the way.
PSALM 25:8 NRSV

Be kind to me so that I may live and hold on to your word.
Uncover my eyes so that I may see the miraculous
things in your teachings.
PSALM 119:17–18 GOD'S WORD

GOD'S LIGHT OF RESTORATION

O God, commander of armies, restore us
and smile on us
so that we may be saved.

PSALM 80:7 GOD'S WORD

As evening falls, the light at the top of the lighthouse tower begins its nightly vigil. It sweeps across the water below, dispelling the darkness and giving confidence and courage to those who pass by during the night. Although the seas are calm, the light provides a deep sense of well-being.

Let God shine His light into your life. It will calm your fears and restore your sweet assurance that all is well. It will give you courage and confidence to carry on even through the long night of your soul. It will flood your heart and remind you that God loves you and is always watching over you.

The light of God's love never fails.

Restore to me the joy of Thy salvation,
And sustain me with a willing spirit.

PSALM 51:12 NAS

I have suffered much, O LORD;
restore my life again, just as you promised.
LORD, accept my grateful thanks and
teach me your laws.

PSALM 119:107-108 NLT

The LORD saves good people;
he is their strength in times of trouble.
The LORD helps them and saves them;
he saves them from the wicked,
because they trust in him for protection.

PSALM 37:39-40 NCV

My Solid Rock

*The L*ORD *is my rock, my fortress,*
and my deliverer, my God,
my rock in whom I take refuge, my shield,
and the horn of my salvation, my stronghold.

PSALM 18:2 NRSV

⌘

The lone structure is visible from a great distance. For years, the stone lighthouse has been a consistent fixture in the seaside community nearby. Through seasons of rain and seasons of sunshine, it never seems to change—a strong fortress in good times and bad.

Is it raining in your life today? Or is the warm sunshine beaming down on your shoulders? No matter what is happening in your life, God is always there. He is a tower of strength, a never-changing fortress, always ready to shine His loving and healing light into your life.

⸙

He is dependable and solid. Place your trust in Him, and He will never fail you.

He alone is my rock and my savior—
my stronghold.
I cannot be severely shaken.
PSALM 62:2 GOD'S WORD

Depend on the LORD;
trust him, and he will take care of you.
PSALM 37:5 NCV

We depend upon the Lord alone
to save us. Only he can help us;
he protects us like a shield.
PSALM 33:20 TLB

GOD'S LIGHT SHINES
THROUGHOUT THE EARTH

Be exalted above the heavens, O God;
Let Thy glory be above all the earth.

PSALM 57:5 NAS

Throughout the night, the light from the lighthouse sweeps across the sea below, penetrating the darkness and encouraging those who pass by. Though the light shines out from the highest point in the harbor, it never abandons its quest to protect those far below on the water.

God our Father sits on His throne high above the earth, but He is always ready to protect and encourage those He has created on the earth below. He is intimately interested in you and in each and every challenge you are facing in your life.

He is determined to help you. You can depend on Him. He will always hear you when you call.

Who is the King of glory?
The LORD strong and mighty,
the LORD mighty in battle.
Lift up your heads, O you gates;
lift them up, you ancient doors,
that the King of glory may come in.

PSALM 24:8-9 NIV

In God is my salvation and my
glory: the rock of my strength,
and my refuge, is in God.
Trust in him at all times; ye people,
pour out your heart before him:
God is a refuge for us.

PSALM 62:7-8 KJV

MY GUIDE IN ANY STORM

Hear my voice in accordance with your love;
preserve my life, O LORD,
according to your laws.

PSALM 119:149 NIV

The night is stormy, and a small craft bobs up and down on the crest of the waves. The men inside are looking for the light that will lead them to safety, but the storm clouds are hanging low. The frightened fishermen fear the light from the lighthouse will not be able to reach them. Exhausted, they almost lose hope. Then they spot the light boring a hole in the dense clouds. Soon they are safely on shore.

Do you feel as if your "little boat" is taking on water? Perhaps you feel weak and alone in the darkness, without hope.

God's light can penetrate the darkest clouds and reach you in the midst of any storm. Look up, for He is your salvation and your hope.

You are a hiding place for me;
you preserve me from trouble;
you surround me with glad cries
of deliverance.

PSALM 32:7 NRSV

I will call to you
whenever trouble strikes,
and you will help me.

PSALM 86:7 TLB

O LORD, keep me alive for the sake of your name.
Because you are righteous, lead me out of trouble.

PSALM 143:11 GOD'S WORD

God is our refuge and strength,
a very present help in trouble.
Therefore will not we fear, though the
earth be removed, and though the mountains
be carried into the midst of the sea.

PSALM 46:1–2 KJV

LORD, I am in great trouble, so I call out to you.
Lord, hear my voice; listen to my prayer for help.

PSALM 130:1–2 NCV

The Source of Power

They find joy in your name all day long.
They are joyful in your righteousness
because you are the glory of their strength.
By your favor you give us victory.

PSALM 89:16–17 GOD'S WORD

ᵒᵖᵒ

A small fishing vessel turns toward shore, yet danger lurks in the darkness just below the waterline—rocks that could tear at the hull and sink the craft and its occupants. The strong beam from the lighthouse reveals the dangers in the path of the small vessel, and the men are able to make their way around the treacherous rocks to the safety of the harbor.

The light of God's presence in your life will give you wisdom and courage. It will reveal the danger that lurks in your path—those things that can sink your hopes and dreams and leave you floundering in the sea of life. Put your trust in Him. He will not fail you.

I can lie down and go to sleep,
and I will wake up again,
because the LORD gives me strength.

PSALM 3:5 NCV

Glory in his holy name;
let the hearts of those who seek the LORD rejoice.
Look to the LORD and his strength;
seek his face always.

PSALM 105:3–4 NIV

Powerful is your arm!
Strong is your hand!
Your right hand is lifted high in glorious strength.

PSALM 89:13 NLT

Save me, O God, by Your name,
And vindicate me by Your strength.

PSALM 54:1 NKJV

O God, Thou art
awesome from Thy sanctuary.
The God of Israel Himself gives strength and
power to the people. Blessed be God!

PSALM 68:35 NAS

May the LORD give strength to his people!
May the LORD bless his people with peace!

PSALM 29:11 NRSV

LIGHT RESCUES FROM DEATH

For Thou hast delivered my soul from death,
Indeed my feet from stumbling,
So that I may walk before God
In the light of the living.

PSALM 56:13 NAS

As a storm rages, a small craft takes on too much water and capsizes. In the blackness of the stormy night, a desperate fisherman clings to the side of his boat, praying for a miracle. Suddenly a light sweeps across his arms. He raises his head and sees that the ocean currents have swept him in the direction of the shore. The ever-vigilant light from the lighthouse has illuminated his plight, and the alarm has sounded. Soon, strong arms are pulling him to safety.

———

Are you feeling alone and hopeless in one of life's raging storms? Look up, for God's light is shining on you. Call out to Him, and He will pull you from the dark waters to safety in His loving arms.

I cannot count the times when you have faithfully rescued me from danger. I will tell everyone how good you are, and of your constant, daily care. I walk in the strength of the Lord God. I tell everyone that you alone are just and good.

PSALM 71:15-16 TLB

In their distress they cried out to the LORD. He rescued them from their troubles.

PSALM 107:6 GOD'S WORD

I will praise you, LORD, because you rescued me. You did not let my enemies laugh at me.

PSALM 30:1 NCV

A MIGHTY FORTRESS

Bow down Your ear to me,
Deliver me speedily;
Be my rock of refuge,
A fortress of defense to save me.

PSALM 31:2 NKJV

The towering lighthouse on the point is a symbol of strength and a constant comfort. Its rock walls are easily visible in the daylight, and its light shines brightly throughout the night into the water. All those who live in the area and those

who pass by in ships know that if they should lose their way, they can scan the horizon for the lighthouse. It is always there, never moving, never changing.

If you feel that you have lost your way, look around you. God is always there—never moving, never changing. He will help you find your way back home.

Commit yourself to the
LORD; let Him deliver him;
Let Him rescue him,
because He delights in him.

PSALM 22:8 NAS

But the LORD is my defender;
my God is the rock of my protection.

PSALM 94:22 NCV

God's way is perfect!
The promise of the LORD has proven to be true.
He is a shield to all those who take refuge in him.

PSALM 18:30 GOD'S WORD

I stand silently before the Lord, waiting for
him to rescue me. For salvation comes from
him alone. Yes, he alone is my Rock, my rescuer,
defense and fortress. Why then should I be
tense with fear when troubles come?

PSALM 62:1–2 TLB

THE ONLY ONE

For who is God save the LORD?
or who is a rock save our God?

PSALM 18:31 KJV

❧

As darkness falls on the shoreline, the light burns brightly from the solitary lighthouse. No houses or other buildings are around this lone structure as it reaches out to the sea and guides ships safely to shore. The lighthouse stands as a solitary beacon of safety and refuge.

Are you looking for something or someone to show you the way to happiness and peace? Only God can provide what you are searching for. He is the one and only true light in our dark world.

⸻ ❦ ⸻

He is the One who stands on the highest point of the harbor and guides you with His light. Trust in Him, and He will never fail you.

I will go in the strength of the Lord GOD;
I will make mention of Your
righteousness, of Yours only.
O God, You have taught me from my youth;
And to this day I declare Your wondrous works.

PSALM 71:16–17 NKJV

I find rest in God; only he can save me.
He is my rock and my salvation.
He is my defender; I will not be defeated.

PSALM 62:1–2 NCV

HE QUIETS MY FEARS

*Yes, he alone is my Rock, my rescuer,
defense and fortress. Why then should
I be tense with fear when troubles come?*

PSALM 62:2 TLB

ach night—whether stormy or clear—the light shines
down from the lighthouse. The beam quietly cuts through the
water and disarms the terrors that lurk in the darkness. Those
who must earn their living from the sea or pass by in the dead
of night depend on the light for their safety. It gives them
courage and confidence.

If fear is lurking just below the surface of your life, put your
trust in God. He will shine His light on you, and soon you will
be rejoicing in the freedom that comes with knowing you are safe in His tender care.

You need never face a stormy sea or the
terrors of darkness alone. He is always
there when you need Him.

Commit your cause to the LORD; let him deliver —
let him rescue the one in whom he delights!

PSALM 22:8 NRSV

O LORD, I have come to you for protection;
don't let me be put to shame.
Rescue me, for you always do what is right.

PSALM 31:1–2 NLT

For the sake of Thy name,
O LORD, revive me.
In Thy righteousness bring my soul out of trouble.

PSALM 143:11 NAS

Rescue me from my enemies, O LORD,
for I hide myself in you.
Teach me to do your will,
for you are my God;
may your good Spirit
lead me on level ground.

PSALM 143:9–10 NIV

Standing Guard

He will cover you with his feathers,
and under his wings you will find refuge;
his faithfulness will be your shield and rampart.

PSALM 91:4 NIV

ᒉᓴ

Throughout the night, the light from the lighthouse sweeps across the sea, revealing the rocks in the water below and guarding the mouth of the harbor from unfriendly intruders. Even in the darkness, the keeper of the lighthouse is able to see the flags of every ship. If danger approaches, he quickly sounds the alarm.

If you are struggling with fear, remember that God is always watching over you. He knows about every storm and every intruder who will ever come into your life. You need not fear, for He is watching.

He never sleeps, and His strong arm is always ready to defend you. Put your trust in Him.

For who is God, except the LORD?
And who is a rock, except our God?
It is God who arms me with strength,
And makes my way perfect.

PSALM 18:31–32 NKJV

You are indeed my rock and my fortress;
for your name's sake lead me and guide me,
take me out of the net that is
hidden for me,
for you are my refuge.

PSALM 31:3–4 NRSV

GOD'S STRENGTH

You divided the sea by Your strength;
You broke the heads of the
sea serpents in the waters.

PSALM 74:13 NKJV

The waves pound the beach and the rocks below the strong tower on the hill. No matter how ferocious they appear, however, the lighthouse stands erect high above them, impervious to their threat. For centuries, it has held its ground for the sake of the ships that pass by in the night.

Are raging waves pounding your life? Like the lighthouse on the hill, God is not intimidated by the angry waves that threaten from below. He is constant, never failing, always ready to come to your rescue. Let Him be the strong tower in your life. Let Him be your refuge from the storm.

Take courage in God's tender love for you. As you walk in His light, He will lead you to higher ground.

Be Thou exalted, O LORD, in Thy strength;
We will sing and praise Thy power.
PSALM 21:13 NAS

You have turned on my light! The Lord
my God has made my darkness turn to
light. Now in your strength I can scale
any wall, attack any troop. What a God
he is! How perfect in every way! All his
promises prove true. He is a shield for
everyone who hides behind him.
PSALM 18:28-30 TLB

Your arm is mighty.
Your hand is strong.
Your right hand is lifted high.
PSALM 89:13 GOD'S WORD

Constant and Sure

But even the darkness is not dark to you.
The night is as light as the day;
darkness and light are the same to you.

Psalm 139:12 NCV

The lighthouse towers over the water below. It is the one constant and sure thing on the landscape. Even before the ships are near enough to see it standing majestically on the highest point of the harbor, their crews know that it is there. It has always been there. Its mission never changes. Its beam never dims. It is their one sure thing.

When the storms of life come your way, do you wonder if God is still there? He is! He has always been there, watching over you, bringing you safely through every sorrow and grief. He is your one sure thing.

Place your trust in Him, and let Him be your strong tower.

When darkness overtakes the godly,
light will come bursting in.
They are generous, compassionate, and righteous.

PSALM 112:4 NLT

He Is Always There

I will declare that your love stands firm forever,
that you established your faithfulness
in heaven itself.

PSALM 89:2 NIV

ↄ℘

The night is cloaked in darkness. The waves beat steadily against the shore. Suddenly the light from the nearby lighthouse cuts through the darkness. It rotates across the water and then vanishes. Though the fishermen do not see the light for a few moments, they know that it is there. They understand that the beam is simply completing its rotation.

As you experience the warmth and security of God's light in your life, remember that He is always with you, even when the light of His presence is not beaming down directly on your path. He is always there.

———

If you wait, His light will come again, washing over you and bringing you peace in the midst of the storm.

It was you who opened up springs and streams;
you dried up the ever flowing rivers.
The day is yours, and yours also the night;
you established the sun and moon.

PSALM 74:15–16 NIV

I, the LORD, am your God,
Who brought you up from the land of Egypt;
Open your mouth wide and I will fill it.

PSALM 81:10 NAS

Call Out to Him

Be Thou to me a rock of habitation, to which I
may continually come;
Thou hast given commandment to save me,
For Thou art my rock and my fortress.

Psalm 71:3 NAS

The towering lighthouse stands as a symbol of security to all those who see it. It does not move from its imposing position on the point. Inside the tower, there is always a keeper on duty, doing whatever is necessary to ensure that the light will be there whenever it is needed.

No matter how great or insignificant your need may be, God is always ready and able to come to your defense. When you call out to Him, He will hear you and flood your troubled waters with the never-failing light of His love.

You can count on Him. He will always be there to see you through every storm.

But I will sing of your strength,
in the morning I will sing of your love;
for you are my fortress,
my refuge in times of trouble.
O my Strength, I sing praise to you;
you, O God, are my fortress, my loving God.

PSALM 59:16–17 NIV

I cried unto thee, O LORD: I said,
Thou art my refuge and my portion
in the land of the living.

PSALM 142:5 KJV

Strength for Battle

Bless the Lord, who is my rock.
He gives me strength for war
and skill for battle.

PSALM 144:1 NLT

Alone in the water, the lighthouse stands on a promenade high above the harbor. At its base, it is surrounded by the sea. To reach this towering structure, the keeper must cross the water in a boat and then climb to the top along a rock path. The faithful keeper grows stronger each day as he climbs to the top of the tower to carry out his duties and do battle with the darkness.

Set your heart and mind to make God your high tower. As you go to Him each day, you will gain strength and courage to fight the battles in your life. You will soon be ready to push back the darkness in your life and let the light of His love shine through.

To declare that the LORD is upright;
He is my rock, and there
is no unrighteousness in Him.

PSALM 92:15 NAS

The LORD has become my stronghold.
My God has become my rock of refuge.

PSALM 94:22 GOD'S WORD

Lead Me Out of Danger

Yes, you are my Rock and my fortress;
honor your name by leading me out
of this peril.

PSALM 31:3 TLB

The lighthouse towers above the sea. Day or night it stands as a firm fortress of strength and a beacon of light. As the sun slips below the horizon, the light from the lighthouse shines down on the water and reveals any potential danger lurking beneath the surface.

No matter what danger lies ahead, the light of God's presence will protect you and keep your life from shipwreck. He stands as an ever-present, never-failing fortress, high above the swirling waves that threaten to dash your hopes and dreams. Put your trust in Him, and let Him lead you away from danger and into the safety of His harbor.

Keep your eyes on the light of His everlasting love, and you will never be disappointed.

The LORD is a stronghold for the oppressed,
a stronghold in times of trouble.

PSALM 9:9 NRSV

Give us help from trouble: for vain is
the help of man. Through God we shall
do valiantly: for he it is that shall tread
down our enemies.

PSALM 60:11-12 KJV

Led Out of Peril

Direct my steps by Your word,
And let no iniquity have dominion over me.

PSALM 119:133 NKJV

In the midst of the storm, the sea grows rough. The swells have great power. They can easily crush a vessel if it is left to drift. In order to protect their boats, the fishermen always keep them tied securely to the dock.

God provides light and protection for all those who ask for His help. Open your heart and cling to His promise. Make sure that your life is tied securely to His. Then you can live in

confidence that His light will be there to protect and guide you to safety even in the midst of the most frightening storm.

Trust Him. He will not fail you.

Lead me in Thy truth and teach me,
For Thou art the God of my salvation;
For Thee I wait all the day.

PSALM 25:5 NAS

Now teach me good judgment
as well as knowledge.
For your laws are my guide.

PSALM 119:66 TLB

Do not be far from me,
for trouble is near
and there is no one to help.

PSALM 22:11 NIV

This and other books in the Psalms Gift Edition™ series are available from your local bookstore.

Lighthouse Psalms

Garden Psalms

Love Psalms

If you have enjoyed this book, or if it has impacted your life, we would like to hear from you. Please contact us at:

Honor Books
Department E
P.O. Box 55388
Tulsa, Oklahoma 74155

Or by e-mail at info@honorbooks.com